First Timers Guide
on **How to Survive** in
New York State Prison

Kemp "Zac" McCoy

Order this book online at www.trafford.com
or email orders@trafford.com

Most Trafford titles are also available at major online book retailers.

Printed in the United States of America.

ISBN: 978-1-4907-1775-3 (sc)
ISBN: 978-1-4907-1776-0 (e)

Trafford rev. 11/13/2013

www.trafford.com

North America & international
toll-free: 1 888 232 4444 (USA & Canada)
fax: 812 355 4082

TABLE OF CONTENTS

PREFACE

In New York state alone, there is an average of 22,000 people who are paroled every year, and over the course of a two year period, approximately 13,200 of those will return to prison. According to reports, it costs approximately $36,000 annually to house a prisoner in New York State, and there is an increase in this figure for those who are ill with ailments. For example, the cost of housing an elderly prisoner is $72,000 annually.

Be clear that this is strictly business. Nothing more, nothing less. Once you understand that you will know how to do your time. Corcraft industries alone generates hundreds of millions of dollars from the public and private sector annually, off of the sweat and cheap labor of it's prisoners in the State of New York. If this sounds familiar to those of you who are historically and culturally aware, it's because it is. This is nothing more than slavery during modern times. The same concepts apply. In here we work for practically nothing. We are stripped of everything, and then taken from our families. If we act up, we get beat and punished. Don't be a fighter or someone that has a problem with being told what to do, or one of those that decides that you want to buck the system, then the end result for those of us like that is not just placing a bullseye on your back, but could possibly be death.

From the legislators viewpoint (in Albany), there is no such thing as rehabilitation to be gained from this corrective process. There is a constant display of this viewpoint in the denial of the majority of prisoners for Work Release, C.A.S.A.T., and Parole. Programs are set up and established solely for the purpose of federal funding, with the public belief that, their intended goal is to uplift "our prisoners," and get them to change their views, actions, behavior and ultimately their lives, to become honest, hard working and productive law abiding citizens. Rightfully so, because in all actuality our focus should be one that wants to become better individuals. So in a sense, the legislators in my opinion, have hit the nail on the head this time, minus the hidden agenda of the construction of certain programs to be eligible for federal funding. However, for rehabilitation, and the embracing of the dynamics of it's concept cannot be obtained unless it comes from within the individual. Change is not something that can be given to a person, if change is not what the person wants.

This is a place that is easy to get into, but hard as hell to get out of. There are so many people in prison that will more than likely never see the streets again, and for those of you with a sentence of life as a maximum with the possibility of parole, here is a little education for you. Life sentences were created to deal with dangerous and uncontrollable individuals who are a threat to the well being of our law abiding society. You'll be able to see that mainly racial and ethnic minorities serve a disproportionate number of life sentences. Two thirds of those of us with life sentences are non white (66%), reaching as high as (93.7%) of the life sentenced population in the State of New York, according to studies. Parole board panels who are seen on a monthly basis, refuse to give long-time prisoners a chance to redeem themselves, and end up denying release to lifers who have been before them six, seven or even eight times or more (for an additional twenty four month hold each time), going way beyond the court imposed punishment for a crime that was committed ten, twenty or even thirty years ago.

For those of you who're my intended audience, allow me to be the first to tell you that there is nothing nice about prison. The hallways are dark, dank and have a very unpleasant smell about them. In here, you will not see many people that will treat you like a human being. In some places, most of the officers talk to you as if you are a child, with you having done nothing to warrant it, and god forbid if you should talk back, or decide that you want to stand up for yourself. You will learn very fast that there is no fairness or justice in prison. You'll be faced with being denied most liberties, and will even be subjected to having another man look into the crack of your ass if you decide you'd like to go on a visit. If this isn't enough, then know that your families, friends and loved ones will be affected by this as well. They too will be subjected to searches and harassment when coming to see you, simply as a deterrent. You will have complete strangers read your mail before you do, and will perhaps deny you that sexy photo that your wife/girlfriend just sent to you without you being allowed to see if the photo was inappropriate or not. Those genuinely innocent photo's that your children sent to you, you probably won't be able to see as well, because the way that they waved to daddy, or mommy, the people in correspondence may feel that the children were throwing up some sort of gang signs. Is this what you want?

Once you get here, for those of you that will be spending your time in a maximum security prison, you will be amongst some of New York State's most notorious criminals. There are guys here who have raped women and children. There are guys here who have raped and murdered entire families. You will even run into the occasional murderer that has killed for no reason at all, not to mention all of the young murderers who are now coming to prison with so much time that their chances of seeing the streets again are slim to none. Some guys you run into that have been here for decades, are not mentally stable, and are considered to be walking time bombs-literally. You will see and/or hear of people dying in here for the smallest things, and you'll probably witness and/or hear of officers killing prisoners occasionally. Again I ask, is this what you want?

Dear reader I beg of you please, if you have time to do, then do your time wisely, and don't allow your time to do you. Take this opportunity, as well as, this blessing (for most of us), to educate yourself and your families. Teach yourself a skill/trade that will place you in a more marketable position upon release. With the recent closing of seven medium and minimum security facilities, I pray that it is an indication that we are doing the best that we can to not only stay out of prison, but realize that our lives, and our freedom hold a lot more value than we have placed on them thus far.

A WORD FROM THE AUTHOR

Life is way too short so, try to value what you may have left of it. Tomorrow is promised to no one, and keep in mind that time spent in prison is time you'll <u>never</u> be able to get back. Sure, you may even learn a valuable lesson in here that you may need to carry you throughout life, but I'm sure you'd rather be free to enjoy life's liberties than to have them stripped from you. Once you are behind these bars and barbed wire, you will <u>never</u> be the same.

Make an assessment of what your life is like right now. Do you have family? Do you have loved ones and children? Do you love them, and are you loved by them? Will you do anything in your power to make sure that they are happy, and that they will be provided for? If you do, then know that you will <u>never</u> be able to do any of those things from here. Know that if you are not there, someone else will be there to be called mommy or daddy, and someone else will be there to give them the happiness and provisions that they'll need.

Dear reader I beg of you, when pushed to the point of wanting to do the wrong thing, think about your loved ones and family cause they're worth it, and place more value on your life cause you deserve it.

THE AUTHOR

INTRODUCTION

I n wanting to take the initiative to share my experiences with you based on being in prison for the last thirty two years, on different occasions, I had to ask myself, "What is it that I could possibly give to a person that may be faced with being incarcerated in a New York State Prison for the first time?"

I have been around some of New York States most notorious and infamous criminals. Everyone from Pappy Mason, Mark Chapman, David Berkowitz, Ronnie Defeo, Gus Faraci, Jerry the Jew, and many more. The list goes on and on. Just as I've been in places like Attica, Auburn, Comstock, Clinton, Elmira, Sing Sing, Sullivan, and more. Make a mental note that no two places are alike, but if you are faced with having to do time, then I will attempt to allow you to gain a pinch of an understanding of what to expect, through my eyes and experiences.

They say that life is what you make it, and this saying is truly applicable to prison, as well as life. Not to put anyone down, most of us go throughout our lives not caring about anything or anyone. The only thing that can awaken someone that has taken everything and everyone for granted, is for that someone to lose what it is that someone has or had. Then and only then can that someone learn to appreciate the blessings that they have been given. Thus, when first contemplating the drafting of this book, the question that arose in my mind was not who would be my intended audience, but "What is it that I could possibly give to the audience that this book is intended for?" That question was quickly answered after reflecting on the past maybe ten years or beyond, as well as, recently through the media watching how many public figures and celebrities are coming to prison for the first time.

WHAT TO EXPECT UPON COMING TO NEW YORK STATE PRISON

B
eing that this book is aimed towards first timers, there are a lot of things that you are going to need to know, if you are going to not only survive, but make your time as close to being comfortable for you as possible. Do not get it confused however, because the last thing you ever want to do is become comfortable with what you are preparing to be faced with. This is not home, for home, where ever that may be, is where you belong. Unless of course, you have astronomical numbers, and if this is the case for you, then this is going to be your home if you'll never see the streets again, then by all means, get as comfortable as you'd like.

Most of us as people tend to take things for granted. Everything from the people in our lives, the blessings that we receive, and even our life, liberty and freedom, which is what led you to this. So, since you know you've taken things for granted most of your life, now is the time to start learning how to be more appreciative of not just life, generally speaking, but those in your life as well, i.e., family, loved ones, etc. You must also go throughout your period of incarceration, however long it may be, knowing that; 1) Tomorrow is promised to no one, and; 2) That there is the possibility that you may lose family members while doing your time. You may even be faced with tragedy's and heck, realistically speaking, you may not even make it out alive yourself, because again, tomorrow is promised to no one.

We go through life on a daily basis clouded mentally by the events and circumstances that take place in our lives on a consistent basis, and the one thing that most of us fail to reflect on is death. Don't, be afraid of the word, just keep in mind that it is the one thing that no one is exempt from, and will happen to each and every one of us, one day.

Remember that you are now a part of a controlled environment that you have absolutely no control over. You have gone from having the liberty of the smallest things like, being able to sleep as long as you'd like to or, running to the store when you'd like to or, taking a shower or bath when you'd like to or, even being able to use the bathroom when you'd like to, to now being told what to do, and where to do it. If this sounds ludicrous to you, it's because it is, and the harshest of realities will only set in once you get here (if your out on bail reading this). If you've already been sentenced and you are here, then know that Riker's Island in no way, will be able to prepare you for what you will be faced with upon entering New York State Prison, for. State Prison is a world of it's own.

Again, remember that you have no control over your now controlled environment, and that applies to the things that happen on the outside as well to your family and loved ones. The sooner you understand that, the less stress you will place upon yourself throughout your period of incarceration. I'm pretty sure that there is some of you that may even leave behind some money that would be helpful to your families and loved ones, but in no way at all can money possibly fix everything once your gone. Money can not produce your physical presence on those nights when your wife or girlfriend is lonely, and need you by their side. Money can not take your children to school and be able to pick them up because your wife or girlfriend's schedule may be hectic that day. Money won't allow you to be there to take your family members to the hospital and sit by their bedside when the circumstances arise. The bottom line is that, money may help them while your gone, and will even help you while your here, but it doesn't mean much if your not there. Let's face it, for if you had that much money, you wouldn't have brought my book, and you definitely wouldn't be in prison.

I know that this may be a hard pill to swallow for some of you, but dealing with incarceration allows you to see things for what they really are. If you have left behind a wife/girlfriend or boyfriend/husband, then know that there are going to be times when she/he will have needs that have to be met, and being that your here, there is absolutely nothing that you can do to meet those needs. Unless of course, you are married and fortunate to be in a prison that offers the Family Reunion Program (Trailer Visits), then you will be able to meet those needs. However, there are times when even this won't keep a woman/man faithful in your absence, for you and only you know what type of woman/man you left behind. In the event you are not fortunate to be married and end up in a prison that offers the Family Reunion Program, then depending on how close your relationship is with the woman/man in your life, especially if she/he is by your side throughout your ordeal every step of the way, and does not neglect you in any form or fashion, then my advice to you is to marry her/him, and give that person what it is she/he deserves when you return to society. Whatever you do, <u>do not</u> allow yourself to stress over matters that you have <u>no</u> <u>control</u> over. Remember what I told you in the beginning how you are now a part of an environment that you have absolutely no control over. Keep in mind that even if your mate has been unfaithful throughout the course of your period of incarceration, not only is there nothing that you can do about it, but again, if she/he has not forgotten you and is by your side, and makes sure that you need or want for nothing while your here throughout your ordeal, then be mature enough to be able to overlook that especially if you are not able to meet those needs that need to be met on an intimate level. Or, you can simply dissolve the relationship in a mature manner, in a worse case scenario. Sounds crazy doesn't it? The bottom line is that, it is what it is.

Once you've entered reception, whether your in a cell, or in a dormitory setting, now is the time to lay in your bunk and reflect on what your life is now, and what you want it to be once released. Dig deep and find out where you went wrong, and know that starting right now, is the time to correct it. Reflect on who and what's important to you, because now is when you'll find out who your friends are and who really cares about you, and after having done this, if what's important to you is still in the street, and you've been taken from it or them, then you will learn from this harsh experience, but if what's left in the street is not important to you then know that if you don't change how you think and act now, then know that there is a permanent cell waiting for you with your name all over it.

BEWARE, for the words in this book at times will be very candid and up front, for my goal is to literally smack you back into reality, and if my intentions in doing so works, then my goal has been accomplished. Remember from my introduction, I wish this experience/nightmare on no one.

CLASSIFICATION

I t is reported through prison grapevine, and statistics that it costs taxpayers forty thousand dollars annually to house, feed and clothe a healthy New York State Prisoner. That figure is strikingly more for elders and the ill among New York State's Prison population. When coming upstate after being shaved, deliced and showered, you will be issued clothes consisting of four pair of green pants, four short sleeve green shirts, one green sweatshirt, one pair of black work boots, one pair of sneakers, one white dress shirt and one green clinker (winter coat). If it is cold there will be no long johns or winter hat, these you must either have your family send them to you or, purchase through the commissary if they are sold, there at reception or your receiving prison/facility or, these things and others can be purchased from a vendor (catalog), as well.

While at your Reception Center (i.e., Downstate, Elmira, Ulster, etc.), here is where you will receive your classification. Whether it will be Maximum, Medium or Minimum security will depend solely upon the length of time you have to serve, as well as how much time you have done already in your county jail. Normally, you will stay in one of these Reception Centers for no longer than a month or two, depending upon bed availability at your approved receiving prison/facility. While at these Reception Centers you are allowed to receive visits and packages, but check with the officers on when your allowed to receive them. In Downstate you are not allowed to receive a package until after thirty days (check into this to be sure because things have more than likely changed since I've been there), and you are not allowed to receive a visit until after two weeks of being in reception, for new arrivals. The rules are probably a little bit different at each Reception Center, but again, check with the officer in regards to the rules governing the visits and packages.

Immediately after arriving at your Reception Center, you will be allowed to call home that evening, and are allowed three trys to get through to your family if your first attempts are unsuccessful. Do not have your family and/or loved ones send you a package immediately until you've found out when you are allowed to receive one, as well as, what you are allowed to have in a package. You can always forward your family and/or loved ones a copy of the directive #4911 that governs what you can and can't have in a package (located in every facilities law library) or, you can have your family go online at www.NYSDOCS.com, and download a copy of the directive #4911 so that you'll save your family and/ or loved ones a lot of time, energy, money and hassle with having to go back and forth with buying things for you, and then you sending them back because they're not allowed at your Reception Center, and your family and/or loved ones end up being stuck with the items you couldn't have or having to take them back to the store. Do your best to make it as easy as possible for your family and/or loved ones when asking for things because it becomes a hassle to have to go from store to store just to do things to meet our needs, and most of us while in here don't have a clue as to what our people on the outside have to go through out there. In order to prevent that from happening be sure to not just be mindful, but educate yourself as to what you can and can't have before sending your family and/or loved ones on a ghost mission, which is what most of us do in here. What that does if done on a constant basis, is force your people to lean towards not going out there shopping for you, which by the way is a lot cheaper as opposed to buying what you need from a catalog (who's prices can sometimes be a little bit exorbitant, depending on what catalog you purchase from). The best advice to give you is to wait until your money is transferred from Rikers Island or, have money sent to your inmate account which will at least give you the opportunity to be able to go to commissary to purchase some items that will hold you until you can receive a package, or get to your receiving facility where you'll be able to get yourself together slowly while getting into your bid. Keep in mind that you still won't want to spend too much because once they call you to pack up, you will not be allowed to pack anything that is opened, except for cigarettes. Be aware, for those of you who have money sent to you while in reception, if you have surcharge or two (which most of you will unless you are able to have your lawyer waive it for you at sentencing), then know that the Reception Center will take all of it from you, credited towards paying your surcharge(s), of course. If you have only one surcharge, then the Reception will only take fifty percent of all incoming monies from the outside, credited towards your surcharge, and if you have two surcharges then the Reception Center will take one hundred percent of all incoming monies credited towards your surcharge. Once your surcharge has been paid then you won't have to worry about the Department of Corrections touching your money unless you receive a misbehavior report (which I will explain later), have restitution charges, child support or, are on your way out the door to be released. Then you will be faced with paying a gate fee of forty dollars, which is a total percentage from whatever you earn or have coming in from family and/or loved ones, that is given back to you upon your release. I'm not sure if you've ever heard the rumor that when you are released from prison that you are given forty dollars and a bus ticket. That used to be the case, but now the forty dollars that you are given is actually your own money removed from your account throughout your period of incarceration.

While in reception you will also receive your time computation sheet that is a series of calculations the Department of Corrections will follow to the letter, that is prepared by the kind folks up in Albany. If there are any inaccuracies dealing with your time computation sheet you can address those inaccuracies to the Inmate Record Coordinator by explaining the inaccuracies, but make sure you have your proof (paperwork) to substantiate your complaint against whatever inaccurate information that is placed on your time computation sheet.

Your time computation sheet will consist of the date that you were received, the Minimum Term (Time to Serve Minimum), which is established according to the sentence the Judge gave you, Maximum Term (Time to Serve Maximum), if you should have an indeterminate sentence and/or a determinate sentence. The Date Sentenced, Original Maximum Expiration Date, Date Declared Delinquent, Date Returned (which more than likely will not apply to you and more than likely won't be included on your time computation sheet, for this entry is solely for Parole Violators). Also included are the Original Parole Eligibility Date, Other State Sentence Date, Date Discharged, Date Reaffirmed, Prior Time Credit, Parole Board Discharge and Post Release Supervision (P.R.S.). Time Owed (Minimum), Time Owed (Maximum), Parole Jail Time (days). Net Time Owed, Limited Credit Time Possible, Supplemental Merit Time Possible, Merit Time Possible, Good Time Adjustment, Good Time Possible, Limited Credit Time Date, Supplemental Merit Eligibility Date, Merit Eligibility Date, Parole Eligibility Date, Parole Hearing Date/Type, Tentative Release Date, Maximum Expiration

Date, Conditional Release Date and T.A.C. Date/Type (Time Allowance Committee) (which is applicable if you've received a Tier III Misbehavior Report (ticket), which I will explain to you later on), and at the disciplinary hearing if it was stated that you lost good time, then once released from the Special Housing Unit (S.H.U.) the Time Allowance Committee will call you to review your record to determine whether they will give you your good time back, either some of it or all of it. Remember, a lot of the above mentioned entry's probably don't apply to you and therefore won't be included on your Time Computation Sheet because you are a first timer. They were listed to give you a general idea as to what the Time Computation Sheet consists of.

WHAT HAPPENS AFTER I RECEIVE MY CLASSIFICATION?

Either prior to, or directly after receiving your classification, you will already have gone through your physical tests, doctor (blood tests, x-rays, etc.), dentist and eye doctor. Your blood will be tested for HIV, Hepatitis, Diabetes, etc., so that the Department of Corrections medical staff will be aware of your medical conditions and how best to medically treat you. If you do have any ailments please be sure to inform them because this file that they are compiling will follow you everywhere. Your blood will also be placed in the DNA databank, which you will be charged fifty dollars for (this is actually one of your surcharges). Also, what will take place while you are at reception are a series of placement tests, such as schooling (Math, English, etc.) to determine where you will be placed once reaching your receiving prison/facility where you will be spending your time in the beginning. If you have a High School Diploma or G.E.D., and/or College Degree, then make sure you inform your counselor when you are called to see her/him so that when you reach the prison/facility where you will be spending your time, they will verify it and you won't be faced with having to go to school. Once the Department of Corrections knows that you don't need schooling they will then recommend programs to you that will assist you while in prison, as well as, enable you to get out of prison as soon as possible (as long as you don't refuse these programs), because every program that is recommended to you will be told to you by your counselor, but will be handed down by the kind folks up in Albany. You'll find out throughout your period of incarceration that everything that happens to you and for you comes from the kind folks up in Albany. Nothing, and I mean absolutely nothing happens in here to you without Albany knowing about it. You won't have to worry about this though until you reach your receiving facility. Some of you will be going to maximum security prisons, some to medium security facilities and some to minimum security facilities, (if there are any still opened). The differences between the security levels, and living in maximum, medium and minimum security will be explained later.

THE DIFFERENCES BETWEEN MAXIMUM, MEDIUM AND MINIMUM SECURITY

I'm sure that most of you reading this book have watched plenty of television and movies prior to coming to prison, where certain types of prisons were portrayed (I myself know because I've seen a lot of them as well). However, there are not many movies that can truly give you a good idea of what life in prison is actually like. Most of these movies are a serious stretch of someone's imagination, and those that border on any facts only give you a birds eye view of what prison is like. There is one movie that comes to mind that gives you a serious closeness to what prison life is really like, and if any of you've seen American Me then, in my opinion this is one movie that gives you a pretty good idea of how prison life really is, especially on a maximum security level. If you haven't seen this movie and are still out on bail, then I suggest that you view this movie and educate, as well as prepare yourself for what you might or might not be faced with. Be mindful though that there is nothing on television or in a movie that can prepare you for life in prison, but again, they do give you a birds eye view of what it's like because what you see in most movies are tales from people who've been there and have actually lived it.

MAXIMUM SECURITY LIVING

This, as far as state prisons go is by far, the worst of the three levels of security. You will not find any other level of security that is on the same level as a maximum security prison. Regardless to how wild you may hear that some mediums are or how crazy Rikers Island used to be, or probably still is. Maximum security living is truly a world of it's own, and as long as you listen to what I tell you on these pages, you'll more than likely be fine. Never will I tell you that absolutely nothing will happen to you while living in a maximum security prison, or a prison/facility on any security level for that matter, because that would not be telling you the truth. Even after listening to me and taking my advice you must understand that if you are faced with having to live in a maximum security prison, then you will possibly be amongst some of New York State's most hardened criminals. One rule I've always lived by while doing time, is to just stay to myself and not associate with too many people. This is easier said than done because you are going to have to associate with someone while here, for you'll be programming and it's obvious that you'll more than likely have questions about what your program may entail. So, I'm going to give you a few rules to live by that if followed, you should be alright. Again, as I stated earlier, for me to tell you that absolutely nothing is going to happen while you are here would not be truthful, but I can guarantee you that if you take my advice, then your problems will be minimal.

Before continuing, you must know that all maximum security prisons are not on the same level. Although they all have their fair share of nonsense going on, as well as violence, but when it comes to the officers, some prisons officers are worse than others. Also, if this makes any sense to you then know that in the prisons where the officers are worse than others, then keep in mind that in practically every prison the 3:00 p.m., to 11:00 p.m. shift has all of the worse officers in the jail so, if you are in a prison where the officers are the worse to begin with, then know that the 3 to 11 shift in those types of prisons are worse, times ten. However, here are a few rules that will <u>definitely</u> keep you under the radar.

STAY AWAY FROM, AND DO NOT TALK TO THE POLICE.

Sure, there are times that you may actually have to speak to them, but be sure to keep it at a minimum. I've seen a lot of first timers make this mistake when first coming to prison. I realize that most of them are scared and they feel as though they are under some type of microscope by the other prisoners, and that maybe somebody will be able to figure out that they are new. Most guys are able to tell that your new, and it's not that you have this new guy smell or something, it's that we are able to witness your actions, which lets us know that you are new. Although someone wanting to try you because you are new may be true, the one thing that you don't want to do is constantly be seen talking to the police. To everyone that may be watching it doesn't just scream first timer, but when another prisoner constantly sees you in the police's face the wrong impression can be made that you might be a rat, (i.e., snitch, cooperator, informer, etc.), which is something you definitely don't want to be said or assumed about you while being in any prison. The police are not your friends. On a whole, they don't like any of us because we as prisoners have gone to their little towns and have corrupted every nook and cranny north of the five boroughs so, don't be fooled into thinking that they are you friends. While you will find that most old timers will not classify you or label you as a rat unless someone has paperwork on you, (i.e., documents that prove you've gotten on the stand and cooperated/testified against someone, etc.), but it is worth mentioning to make sure that you keep your police contact at a minimum because on the flip side is that you have most of the younger generation that doesn't follow the old school format/ rules, and will not only call you a rat to your face, and/or behind your back, but will fix you up something decent behind it.

DO NOT TAKE ANYTHING FROM ANYONE.

You are now, or soon will be a part of an environment where the criminal mind does not sleep. The people that you are going to be around thrive on not just you being a first timer, but any one that they can trap into their little schemes, cons, etc, etc. Most schemes are a form of subtle extortion, just a way to get into someone's pocket, which at times can be deadly if the recipient of the con is a stand up person. This is why most of these type of people will target new comers or patiently wait for someone that's been there for a while to get caught slipping and show some sign of weakness, and then move in for the kill. There are many reasons that I could give you why not to take anything from anyone, but always keep in mind that ninety nine percent of the people that you encounter throughout your period of incarceration have an ulterior motive, and to keep yourself out of trouble, just do without if you don't have it. Although things have changed drastically since I first came to prison in 1979, but back then there were a number of things that a first timer had to beware of. Booty bandits were the majority of the population, and they were always on the look out for someone to victimize or fresh bait. Most new guys would come into their cell for the first time upon arriving at a prison and find cigarettes, cakes, candies, etc., on their bed and think that they genuinely had a friend somewhere in the prison that must have found out that they just arrived and sent them some goodies. This my friends, is far from the truth. Those goodies were placed there by some bandit that is just waiting to see what you've done with the goodies he's left on your bed. It sounds weak right?, but this is what it used to be like. Believe me when I tell you that once you open or eat anything left on your bed or in your cell, you now belong to him or, if you are a stand up person you are definitely going to need a knife within the next few days because this bandit will be coming to find out what you are made of. The best advice that I can give you is if this should happen to you, say nothing, just simply give him his shit back when he gets there, case closed. Or if you are a stand up person and have no problem with doing what you have to do, then by all means enjoy your goodies and when it's time, handle your business. The best way to avoid any nonsense is to just do without if you don't have it because. it can lead to problems that you might not want.

DO NOT DISCUSS YOUR CRIME WITH ANYONE.

There are a lot of people that probably will already know why you are here, especially if your case was highly publicized. There are so many people in the system that read the daily papers, and listen to the news daily, and will hear the name of a person that has recently committed a crime and will never forget that name or case. They also have in every prison what's called a change sheet that lists all changes daily within the prison, as well as, who is coming to or leaving the prison. So, they know who's coming even before they actually get to the prison, and then, you have the guys that work in the prison law library that read the daily law journals who keep up with the recent changes in the law, and if a case interests them or sticks out they're able to access that case through the most recent legal publications. This means that most guys already know about you as I previously stated, if your case was highly publicized. If you have a heinous crime (i.e., rape, murder/rape or something involved with hurting women and children), then there is a possibility that you may have a hard time. Although you may not have seen it on Rikers Island, or you might have, know that it's very rare to run into a person that has that serious criminal mentality on Rikers Island, but know that when you arrive at a maximum security prison the criminal mentality and activity is most definitely wide awake. You have prisoners there that have been in prison for five, ten, fifteen, twenty, twenty, twenty five, and even thirty years and beyond, and the more you tell or discuss, the more that can be used against you. The best advice that I can give anyone as a first timer is that it's nobody's business why you are in prison so, keep your business to yourself.

IF YOU HAVE MONEY ON THE OUTSIDE KEEP IT TO YOURSELF.

Please, I can not be more clear when I tell you to keep your mouth shut about your finances. Sure, I've told you about the booty bandits. I've told you about the numerous majority of prisoners with the criminal mentality that lie in wait for an opportunity to get into someone's pocket, but I haven't told you about the wolves. The differences between the bandits, the prisoners with the criminal mentality and the wolves is that, the bandits want to fuck, no more, no less. Those with the criminal mentality have a little finesse about their scheming for they only want to get into your pockets, but the wolves have no finesse at all. I will not confine this type of individual to just being a part of a gang (who have the mentality that if they don't eat, then no one else does), but these type of individuals can be lone wolves as well. They don't even have to be told that you have money because there are ways to tell if a person has it or not. Your able to tell by what a person wears on a daily basis. Your able to tell by a person constantly being called to the package room. One of the most watched things by wolves is how much money you spend every time you go to commissary. Be careful on how you spend, and what you get sent in from the streets. Keep it at a minimum and believe me when I tell you that if you do so, you may not have to worry about many problems. There is a flip side to this coin and what I mean by that is, once the wolves have their claws in you it's very hard to be freed from their clutches. Don't get me wrong, for if you are a stand up person and it is in your DNA/make up to defend you and yours at all costs regardless of consequences or repercussions, then by all means live and do you, but if you are not cut from that cloth, then know that once you are a target, anything can happen. What I mean by that is anything from paying every time you go to commissary, to getting packages sent in to them. You'll even find yourself paying their drug debts, and being forced to get on the phone and have money sent to them, and you will not be dealt with or handled in a nice manner, trust me. If this should happen to you then you obviously are not the stand up type so, it's sad to have to tell you that your options are not many. You can sign into protective custody, which will not only place you in a worse position because you are now considered a snitch for in order to sign into protective custody you have to sign in by giving the name of the person or people that's threatening and/or extorting you. I am not advocating any violence here, but it is something that <u>everyone</u> respects. Please do not get it twisted because I do not condone snitching in no form or fashion, but I will tell you that I believe that you should <u>always</u> stand up and be a man, and let no one take anything from you, period. A sincere word of advice is to just keep it simple, that way you stay under the radar, which by the way, is the safest way to travel while doing your time, especially if you know that you are not a warrior. This advice is to not put anyone down, but we are being honest here, and honesty requires for us to realize who you are as an individual, and be totally honest within yourself. Then and only then will you be able to know what lane you belong in and be able to stay within your lane because if you are not built a certain way and decide that you may want to step outside of your lane, there is a possibility that someone will eventually call your bluff and not only pull your card, but fix you as well. Remember dear reader, we are not playing a game of poker in here, we're playing the game of life, period.

YOU MUST KNOW THE THREE THINGS NOT TO DO WHILE YOU ARE HERE.

Here are three rules to remember, while not just being housed in a maximum security prison, but in <u>any</u> prison, that will keep you out of any of the nonsense that the majority of the prisoners thrive on.

STAY AWAY FROM THE DRUGS.

In almost every prison there is someone that always gets drugs in whether it is heroin, marijuana, cocaine, angel dust, pills, etc. Their money is made off of the population, and those who use within that population. Selling drugs in prison can be a very lucrative business because everything that is on the market goes for double the amount that you would normally pay for it on the outside. For example, if you pay ten dollars for a bag of heroin in the streets, then buying it in prison is going to cost you double that amount. Be clear that when you pay the twenty dollars you will only receive half of the bag you would receive out on the streets if you had paid the ten dollars. Guys that hustle in prison will take a New York ten dollar bag and make two jail bags out of it, and will sell each jail bag for twenty dollars a piece. So, if a person wanted to buy a New York bag, then it would cost him forty dollars, maybe more, maybe less. Most guys who don't have the money in their account to pay their bill will normally have someone on the outside take care of their tab/debt for them on a street level, but that can become dangerous after a while. Always remember, you can wear a pair of shoes on a regular basis, and eventually you will wear them down. You can drive a car every day for a couple of years, and eventually it will get tired, and no longer perform. Well, this is the same way prisoners families and loved ones begin to feel on the outside from sending money to this address, and sending money to that address year after year until they eventually get tired and no longer want to do it. One day you will call instructing them to send a hundred dollars to an address and they will tell you sure, we'll take care of it, and it won't get done because they're tired of it. You walk away confident that it will get done because your family has been doing it for you, and now you know that the guy that you owe is expecting the money within the time frame expected. When that money doesn't arrive at the address you were given within the time frame allotted then there is a penalty attached to the initial debt with the understanding that you only have a certain amount of time for that total amount to be at that address given to you. You tried calling, and calling your family to find out what happened, but haven't been able to get through. Finally you start to worry and the initial debt and the attached penalty doesn't make it to the address that you were given, and now the guy wants to hurt you. Once that happens, you will more than likely end up getting hurt (i.e., stabbed, cut, etc.), and sent to protective custody. This is not something that a person needs while doing his time. If drugs are what your into then I suggest that you wait until you get out because, if you're fortunate to be able to pay your debts/ bills, you'll still have to worry about the pee pee man, who comes around randomly or because of suspicion or, because someone was jealous and dropped a slip on you, and when the pee pee man comes he comes unannounced and unexpected. So, unless you are willing to purposely jeopardize your freedom, my advice to you is to just stay away from it for your main objective is to get out of prison, not do something that will keep you in here.

STAY AWAY FROM THE GAMBLING.

This is another major no-no. Keep in mind that if you won't play about your money in the streets then know that <u>no</u> <u>one</u> is willing to play about their money in prison. There are some people that have absolutely no one on the streets, and rely on the money they make in programs, as well as their little side hustles, whatever they may be. Those of you that like betting on sporting events, playing poker, etc., then know that this is just another way for someone to be able to get into your pocket, and once a smart hustler gets into your pocket there's a possibility that you may never get out debt. Sure, on one hand you'll have those that are financially able to pay off forty or fifty packs of cigarettes (some debts can be that high), especially when it comes to playing poker or placing a bet on anything, for often times most people bet with their hearts and not with their wallets. But, on the other hand you'll have those that can not afford to pay such a debt, but will still allow themselves to dig that deep of a hole. When people are faced with such a debt there are only a few ways to handle a person like that. Either he'll get seriously hurt, and this method of handling something like that doesn't make sense to me because if you owe me forty packs of Newports at eight dollars plus a pack, why would I hurt you. If I do so then that only means that you'll be moved out of the jail, and if you tell that I'm the one that hurt you then I'll end up in the box for about a year or more, and the bottom line is that I won't get paid. No, I would rather have you pay me over a long period of time because I already know that you can't afford forty packs so, I'll three, four or five pack you to death until you've finally paid me. So, remember that there are people in here that have no one on the outside and thrive on trying to stay in someone's pocket. Just imagine having three or four people that owe you forty packs of Newports, and you decide that you don't want cigarettes, but instead want food from commissary, and you have each guy get you three or four packs of cigarettes worth of food each commissary until you are paid in full. It just makes more sense to me to have a few guys pay me twenty five dollars a piece each commissary for a couple of months instead of hurting them. So, all in all, be careful with the gambling because sure it has it's rewards at times, but it's losses and pains are far greater than it's rewards. Remember, not every prisoner has that attitude when it comes to debt and may not even be a thinker, which means he may want his money right then and there, and if you don't have it, there may be some serious problems. To avoid this, just stay away from the gambling and you won't have to worry about giving someone your commissary every time you go to the store every two weeks.

STAY AWAY FROM THE HOMOSEXUALS

You'd think that with the scare of HIV/AIDS going on on the outside that it would be a deterrent for those who promote same sex interaction in prison to want to stay away from that practice. The sad reality is that the Department of Corrections does not pass out condoms to assist in the practice of safe sex amongst prisoners, which would be condoning rape in prison as well, sexual assaults, etc., but it still goes on in some prisons. If this is your cup of tea, then by all means go for it, and don't worry about playing russian roulette with your life. Still, I urge you to be safe if it is.

Recently within the last few years or so, the Department of Corrections has included in the inmate rule book a sexual assault charge which not only falls into the category of being one of the gravest offenses that can be committed while in prison, and is classified on the tier system as being a top level (Tier III) offense, whose penalty is probably warranting at· least a year in a Special Housing Unit (S.H.U.), but is a clear indication that it's practice is still very much in existence.

I would like to tell you that you'll more than likely only witness this practice behind the wall, but unfortunately I am unable to do so. This is something you'll also witness in a medium security facility as well.

I first came to prison during a time when it was rampant (Late 70's-Early 80's), and the bandits then would hone in on their targets. Some of them had the aggressive approach, and some had the subtle approach. Those with the subtle approach would befriend you and perhaps even work out and eat with you, and try to slide in through the door of friendship. Then you had the aggressive ones that would approach you in a number of blatant ways. Some bandits would approach a person with two knives, keeping one for himself, and throw the other knife at the feet of their mark, continuing with whatever dialogue. Then you had bandits like Motherdear (M.D.), that would walk up to someone's cell and literally tell a guy, "put your dick on the gate, and it better be there when I get back." Back then whenever a person encountered a sick guy like that, with that frame of mind and aggressiveness, it didn't matter to him and bandits like him if a guy fought back or not. Of course, this didn't apply to everybody, because as I told you before, these bandits honed in on and carefully selected their targets.

There are so many stories that I could tell you that would scare you to death. There were some gay bandits like Motherdear, that were so good with their hands that they would approach some of their targets and knock them out, and when the guy woke up his dick would be in the gay bandit's mouth. Or like the bandit that would run into a guy's cell when the cell door opened, hoping to catch the guy sleeping/slipping, and close the cell door behind him and pull out his knife and may the best man win. If the guy loses and the bandit wins, then the guy will lose more than a fight. So, I think you get the picture, and as I expressed to you before that I'm not going to pull any punches with you, for I want you to not only know how serious prison life is, with the hopes that you will learn to respect your life, liberty and freedom when you are returned back to it. Know that there is no one that you can call to help you because there is no one that is going to hear your cry, for you have just entered the jungle of steel where you have to learn to stand up for yourself. I'm sure that we've all heard the cliche, "Only the strong survive." In here it's not a cliche, it's a reality.

I brought this issue to your attention because there are some prisoners in here that do indulge with this type of activity and take it very serious. I say they take it very serious because there are still marriages being held in certain prisons (under the radar of course), and I'm pretty sure that the last thing you would want is to have someone chasing you around the yard trying to stab you because you were messing around with his prison wife. As I previously stated if it it your cup of tea, then by all means, how can I stop you. I am only trying to educate you, and can't force you to do anything. Play at your own risk, which is all I can tell you on this one.

MEDIUM SECURITY LIVING

There is a <u>huge</u> difference between living in a maximum security prison, and a medium security facility. Aside from the obvious reasons from where the forty foot wall is no longer there, to no longer being in a cell, to now being surrounded by a fence with free movement. There are however, a few medium security facilities that have cells within them, but not many.

Once you arrive at a medium security facility you are able to automatically tell the difference. Being in a maximum security prison there is tension in the air on a regular basis, that you can feel as soon as you get off of the bus. Not saying that you won't experience that tension being in a medium security facility, but it's not the same. You'll be able to feel that tension when something happens throughout the facility, but in comparison to maximum security prison where the tension is felt mostly all of the time, you can tell the difference. There is a far more serious atmosphere and mentality in maximum security prisons as opposed to the playful, nonchalant and care free attitude of the prisoners you see in a medium security facility. One of the things that are taboo behind the wall is sneak thieving, which is something that you'll probably see a lot of in most medium security facilities. Behind the wall there is an unwritten rule that if you are a sneak thief and you decide you'd like to ply your trade do not and I repeat, do not get caught, because if you do, you will seriously get hurt. Again, there is a huge difference between living in a maximum security prison, and a medium security facility, and for those of you that make it to a medium security facility from behind the wall hold your head and keep in mind, the same rules of survival apply.

As I've given you the cardinal rules to live by in a maximum security prison, then know that those same rules apply everywhere you are sent. As I previously stated, there is a huge difference between the two levels of security, but once you've had the chance to experience it, you will be able to live and survive anywhere. There is a certain element that maximum security living automatically gives most of us, and in all actuality it teaches you how to be a man. I used to say many years ago that, the Department of Corrections should make it mandatory where every person that has to do time, must go through a maximum security prison first before going anywhere else. Why?, because in the majority of these medium security facilities that serious element is missing. You see more people acting like children and doing childish things, and I'm not just talking about young guys either. So, in my opinion, I believe that everyone should have to experience going through a maximum security prison because it prepares you for life and survival, and again, teaches you how to be a man.

Nine out of ten medium security facilities you see are based on the same design. We call them cookie cutters. They are pre-fab, quickly constructed, cubicled, dormitory structures that can house either ninety people, or more between the A and B side, depending on how the administration sets the dorms up. Forty five to fifty people per dorm means that everyone has their own single cube, but if there are bunk beds than that increases the number of prisoners that can be housed in that dorm. You'll have some medium facilities that are cooking facilities possessing stoves, ovens, etc., where you will be able to have your own pots and pans. Then you'll have some medium facilities that aren't cooking facilities, and you will only be allowed a plastic hot pot to do your cooking out of. The one disadvantage that you will be faced with in a medium security facility is that there are not as many programs as there are in a maximum security prison, depending which medium security facility you are sent to. You'll find, in most medium security facilities, more voluntary programs than you will regular programs (i.e., Narcotics Anonymous, Alcoholics Anonymous, Public Speaking Workshops, Theater Workshops, Parenting Classes, etc., again depending where you are sent). Take advantage of the programs that are provided for you, whatever they may be, especially if they can assist you with becoming a better person and prepare you for life on the outside.

MINIMUM SECURITY LIVING

There is not much that I can tell you about minimum security facilities because as of recently (2010-2011), most of them have been closed down. I will give you a brief understanding of what they are like based on my research and personal experience, in case there are a couple scattered around that are still open, in the event that one of you should happen to be classified as minimum security.

I'm told that most minimums held no walls nor fences, and I have to take that as being valid information. I remember going on a medical trip when I was in Adirondack medium security facility, and we had to go through Camp Gabriel (A minimum security facility), which is no longer open. I noticed that when we got to Camp Gabriel we drove right into the compound, stopped in front of one of the buildings. The transportation officer got out and minutes later came back with a prisoner, placed him in the van and we continued to drive straight through the compound without stopping or going through one fence or checkpoint. Most people that have been in minimum security facilities have told me that there is usually a little fence around the facility that is not used to keep the prisoners from getting out, but to keep the towns people from getting in (crazy right).

These facilities don't have the commonly seen programs that every other prison/facility offers for these minimum facilities are strictly work camps, where the prisoners all have outside clearance, and the majority of all of their work is done in the town that these facilities are housed in. These prisoners do everything from chopping down trees, cleaning highways, distribute food during emergencys, to removing debris from someones front yard. Basically speaking, these minimums were just free labor provided to the community that these facilities were housed in by the Department of Corrections. As previously stated, mostly all of them are closed with the exception of Beacon (Minimum for women), and whatever one or two that have remained open.

Again, there is not too much to tell you concerning these types of facilities because more than likely, by the time you read this the majority of the minimum security facilities will have been closed.

TRANSFERS

In dispensing information to you about transfers, I myself have recently learned that things have changed so much when it comes to transfers, that I honestly don't believe that Albany knows what it is doing half of the time. However, I will give you a brief view of what transfers entail based on my understanding.

Don't quote me, but there was a time when you could stay in a prison/facility for two years, or·in a hub for the same period of time, disciplinary free, and be able to request to go to whatever prison/facility you wanted to go to. Then that changed to where we are no longer able to request the prison/facility of your choice, to now being able to only choose a certain hub that you'd like to go to, and only Albany knows what prison/facility you will end up in. Albany's only concern is that you ended up in the requested hub. This practice is what is going on now as of the writing of this book.

When wanting a transfer, bring it to your counselor's attention during one of your quarterly's (every three month visit to your counselor), as well as, your counselor will inform you that you are transfer eligible when Albany decides so. Normally we are allowed to be transferred while in a maximum security prison to another maximum security prison outside of the hub that you are in within one year after being in that prison, inside of that hub. Every six months while in a maximum security prison to somewhere within the same hub you are in, providing that there are more maximum security prisons within the hub you are in. The same should apply to medium security facilities as well, for being allowed to go to another medium security facility, within the hub you are in every six months, but as I said in the beginning, things have changed so much that it is difficult for even me to give you something concrete. Do the best you can to educate yourself on this because education is the key to every aspect in prison, and in life.

In anything that you may experience while in prison, realize that your families and loved ones are your voice. Them being on the outside, and being able to make noise from the streets through phone calls, letters, etc., we are able to move mountains. So, when it is necessary, make sure that you don't just explore your options when dealing with something, but learn to utilize your resources because our families and loved ones voices from the outside are very powerful. Most prisoners don't understand this, and therefore never educate their families about the power that they possess.

THE THREE TIER DISCIPLINARY SYSTEM

T his implies just what it states. This three tier system is what is used to penalize prisoners for the infractions that we commit. This system, which is devised by Albany, is what classifies the offenses that prisoners commit, and based on the offense committed, it will determine how much time, if any, a person will receive in a Special Housing Unit (S.H.U.). The law also governs this three tier disciplinary system, and is covered by Chapter Five, Title Seven of the New York Codes Rules and Regulations (N.Y.C.R.R.). Under this law, it is described and broken down as to prisoners rights when this three tier disciplinary system is implemented against any prisoner, and it explains what a prisoner can and cannot expect to happen at a disciplinary hearing. In every prison/facility law library, there is a copy of N.Y.C.R.R., be sure to ask the law clerk to obtain a copy of N.Y.C.R.R. governing disciplinary hearings. Everything as of recent, in all prison/facility law library's have been placed on computer so you'll be able to review, on your own, N.Y.C.R.R., and the chapters that will enlighten you as to what you can expect if you are faced with a disciplinary infraction.

There are three levels of disciplinary classification that determine the punishment given to a prisoner for the offense(s) committed, ranging from the least to the most severe. Each prisoner will receive a rule book upon entering a prison/facility that gives you a listing of all rules and the level/degree of seriousness that comes with it. Once a misbehavior report is issued against a prisoner, it will be reviewed by a reviewing officer, who is usually a Lieutenant, who then places a level of seriousness on each misbehavior report based on the rules that govern each prisoner in New York State. Once you are found guilty of a rule broken it can result in a number of impositions, as well as, the encumbrance of five dollars from your account. This is applied to only two levels of the three tier system once a prisoner is found guilty of an offense, which are of the more serious levels. At the lowest level, a person can be found guilty and not have the $5.00 encumbrance removed from his account because it only applies to the two more serious levels. This $5.00 encumbrance that is taken from your account once a person is found guilty of an offense committed "reportedly" goes towards some sort of officers fund inside of the prison that you are housed in. Don't hold me to this one because as I previously stated, it "reportedly" goes toward this fund, for I'm not 100% sure. For what purpose it serves and why this is so, I don't have a clue.

TIER ONE

This is the lowest level of offenses, whose punishment is minimal. Having a tier one can also result in a Counsel and/or Reprimand. This type of disciplinary hearing is conducted by a Sergeant, and can be appealed to the Superintendent of whatever prison/facility you may be in within twenty four hours of the disposition rendered at your disciplinary hearing. This low level of hearing can not be appealed to the Commissioner as you will find one of the other high level of offenses can be.

A tier one's punishment will exceed no more than thirteen days which can include loss of all or part of all recreation for up to thirteen days. Punishment also includes loss of one commissary buy, except for the items on the facility's commissary sheet that a prisoner needs relating to hygiene or health. Also included are the withholding of a prisoner's radio or packages (with the exception of anything that may be included in that package that may be considered perishable items) or, any two of the dispositions can be imposed. With the disposition of all penalties imposed against us, when it comes to receiving packages already mailed, and ordered, there is a five day grace period that should be adhered to. Meaning, if you ordered a package from a vendor today, and receive a disposition for whatever amount of time, you then have five days to receive that package. If in the event that you don't receive that package within that five day grace period, then you will not receive it. More than likely the package room will send it back, at your expense of course. This five day grace period does not apply to a person that is sent to S.H.U. as a result of a disposition because you can not receive a package in the box. However, keep in mind that there are hidden exceptions to this and any rule, because I have ordered a package and then ended up going to the S.H.U., and when the package came it was placed in my property until I was released from S.H.U. Lastly, included can be the implementation of a work task per day outside of your regular program hours for a period not to exceed seven days in whatever area designated which would either be in a prisoners housing unit or another area in the prison/facility designated for work tasks. This low level of offense can not stop your transfer, nor can it affect your conditional release date (C.R.), as I will explain in the two higher levels of offense. You can further be able to educate yourself as to Tier I misbehaviors by reviewing Chapter Five, Title Seven of the New York Codes Rules and Regulation, part 252.

TIER TWO

This is the next level of tier violations, being a little more serious than Tier I violations. As I previously expressed, being found guilty of a tier two violation can result in a mandatory $5.00 encumbrance from your account, along with whatever disposition imposed by the hearing officer. The other punishments that result from being found guilty of a tier two misbehavior report are; Counsel and/or Reprimand. There is also, as in Tier I disposition(s), the imposition of one work task per day for up to seven days, as well as, the loss of one or more specific privileges for a period of up to thirty days. Usually when you are found guilty of a tier two, the hearing officer will usually impose thirty days loss of phone privileges. Most hearing officers conducting tier two disciplinary hearings will usually take your packages, phone and commissary privileges because they are things that will automatically affect and hurt you. Most times the hearing officer will take your recreation as well, but not being able to go to the yard will not hurt you as much as the loss of packages, phone and commissary. You also have as a disposition the loss of visiting privileges with a particular person where you have had an involvement of improper conduct with a particular person on the visiting room floor. There is confinement to a cell or Special Housing Unit (S.H.U.) on certain days or certain hours for a period of up to thirty days, which you will rarely see done anymore these days. Now a days if you are found guilty of a tier two misbehavior report that calls for time in an S.H.U., you will be sent to an S.H.U. for the time imposed, especially if you are in a medium security facility. If you are in a maximum security prison, the hearing officer will just place you on keeplock status for a period of up to thirty days, and loss of packages, phone and commissary for that period imposed. Under those keeplock circumstances a hearing officer can impose loss of recreation, but mandated by the courts, you are still entitled to one hour of recreation per day while on loss of recreation under keeplock status. In a S.H.U., and at some point throughout the day while you are on keeplock, the one hour recreation period will be afforded to you. Just remember to inform the officer in the morning that you want recreation for that day.

Under the tier two disciplinary dispositions it can also be imposed the loss of special privileges such as facility festivals. Every year most prisons/facilities have festivals and religious festivals as well, whose tickets are sold in the commissary, where prisoners are allowed to invite their families and loved ones to attend the festivals to enjoy music, food and each others company as well. As a result of a disposition, a prisoner can be disqualified from participating in a facility festival, if so imposed by the hearing officer, even if you've paid your money for the festival already. For those of you that are fortunate enough to be able to participate in the Family Reunion Program (trailer visits), know that the disposition of a tier two can affect your trailer visit date if you already have one. For example, if you are in a maximum security prison and you have been placed on keeplock for what ever reason and let's say that it's the first day of March. You will then receive your misbehavior report (ticket) within twenty four hours after being placed on keeplock. Hypothetically speaking, if your trailer date is set for the fifth day of March, you would be allowed to attend your trailer visit even if you haven't gone to your hearing yet to receive the disposition. Let me give you another scenario. Let's say you get placed on keeplock as in the above example, and your trailer visit date is for the twenty third of March, then you are called for your hearing around the seventh day after you were placed on keeplock. After you've gone to your hearing and you were given twenty one days loss of packages, phones and commissar, you <u>will</u> <u>not</u> be able to participate on your trailer date on the twenty third day of March because you were given twenty one days as a disposition. If you are a participant in the Family Reunion Program and you catch a slug (misbehavior report-ticket), and are given anything over twenty one days as a disposition, you <u>will</u> <u>not</u> be able to participate in the Family Reunion Program because a disposition of twenty one days and more will disqualify you from participating. When participating in the Family Reunion Program, and you are faced with a keeplock/misbehavior report and the disposition is less that twenty one days, you will still be allowed to participate in the program, but twenty one days or more and you will be disqualified from doing so.

There is also the imposing of restitution charges for what ever damage a prisoner may have caused to state property that will not exceed $100 dollars. Again, further education of what this section entails can be found under Chapter Five, Title Seven of the N.Y.C.R.R. part 253. Please note that this level of offense can affect your parole board decisions, C.A.S.A.T. decisions, and Work Release decision as well. Once found guilty of a Tier II offense, it can be appealed to the Superintendent within seventy two hours of the disposition and can not be appealed to the Commissioner.

TIER THREE

This level of misbehavior is far more serious than the previous two levels. The tier three disciplinary hearing is conducted by a Captain or someone higher in authority, or an employee designated by the Superintendent. Normally when a person catches an infraction for Tier III he is nine times out of ten automatically keeplocked pending the disposition (behind the wall), just as in a tier II misbehavior. In a medium facility, where you will usually be sent to the S.H.U., or nowadays they have the S-block 200's which are double bunk box cells with two men in each cell that possesses everything within that cell. You have inside of this cell a toilet, sink, bunk beds, shower, window and a recreation pen. So, you literally don't have to come out of this cell for much. The reason a person won't automatically be keeplocked and/or sent to an S.H.U. when a tier III is involved is if he has been given a walking tier III. A walking tier III is mostly what it implies. It is when you have been given a tier III misbehavior report for whatever reason, and you were not sent to an S.H.U. (as in a medium facility), nor were you placed on keeplock (as in a maximum security prison) pending the disposition. It is not that these are rare because you see it all of the time so, when you do hear it happening to someone don't, and I repeat, don't automatically assume the worse about a person, especially if you don't know the particulars. I know how some prisoners develop the bad habit of being judgmental in their thinking and will automatically come to the negative conclusion that a person may be a snitch or something else that could possibly defame a persons character based on a situation like that. Nevertheless, as I stated above, it is something that happens, however rare it may be seen so, never allow yourself to get caught up into the frame of mind of placing a negative stigma on someone without having something tangible as proof.

Tier III hearing dispositions are governed by the same Chapter Five, Title Seven of N.Y.C.R.R. part 254, that informs you of what your rights are at a tier three disciplinary hearing, and what you can and can not expect to happen at a tier three Superintendent's hearing. Some of the dispositions that are applied under this section can include; Counsel and/or Reprimand (although I've never seen this happen under a tier III before), and the mandatory $5.00 encumbrance as under the tier two dispositions. You have the loss of one or more privileges for a specified period of time. Correspondence and/or visiting privileges can also be withheld with a particular person that you have been found guilty of, or had any connections with dealing with improper conduct visit wise or inappropriate correspondence with such a person. There is also the imposition of restitution for the loss of or intentional damage to state property. Unlike the tier two dispositions where the restitution dispositions value would not exceed $100 dollars, in a tier three disposition the monetary damage/value to state property will more than likely exceed $100 dollars. There is the imposition of one work task per day for up to seven days, and for those of us that after being sent to an S.H.U. that still choose to be a problem and/or disruptive while in S.H.U., there is implementation and assignment to a restricted diet for a specified period. This diet which isn't really a diet at all, for the only thing that I feel that could possibly classify this restricted diet as a diet is the fact that you won't receive a regular meal as everyone else will while you are on this diet. No, this restricted diet isn't that easy. You'll still get fed three times a day, but what you will be given will be something that you definitely won't be prepared for. Once given this restricted diet it will only be for a specified period of time, which will actually be entirely up to you because you will have to be evaluated by a Lieutenant or Captain every ten days or so, who will determine if you should be taken off of the restricted diet. You will be checked to see how much weight you've lost, and they have the power to recommend that you be taken off or if he's not satisfied that your ready to be removed off of the restricted diet, then you can write the Superintendent explaining that you've changed and that you are now ready to be taken off of the restricted diet. What is this restricted diet your probably asking? Picture a very bland loaf of bread with carrots and cabbage baked right into the loaf, or the cabbage will be placed in a cup on the side. You will have to eat this for three times a day for however long you allow yourself to stay on this restricted diet. Again, it is entirely up to you how long you stay on this diet. Trust me when I tell you that this loaf of bread is unlike any loaf of bread you've ever eaten. Two weeks of this diet, and either you'll start to enjoy it or be begging to be taken off of it. Keep in mind that the rules pertaining to this issue have probably changed since I was in the box (S.H.U.), and can probably be a lot different. But, this is not something I'm sure you will want to find out about.

One of the most hurtful aspects of the tier three Superintendent's hearing is the losing of good time. There are times that a hearing officer at a tier three Superintendent's hearing will state as a disposition that he recommends loss of good time which is not something that should alarm you, but if the hearing officer tells you for example that he is rendering a disposition of 365 days S.H.U., 365 days loss of packages, 365 days loss of phone privileges, 365 days loss of commissary and 365 days loss of good time, now is the time for you to be alarmed. This means that when it comes time for your conditional release date that you are supposed to be released on (for those of you that may have a determinate sentence), then you won't be released because you lost 365 days of good time which means that you will go home 365 after your initial conditional release date. However, everyone that loses good time goes to a Time Allowance Committee prior to their conditional release date approaching and this committee determines how much of your good time they want to give you back. There are a number of factors considered by this committee to determine how much good time they will give back to you. Some of the main things considered are what your disciplinary record has been like since you were released from S.H.U., how was your program participation, and overall performance since being back in general population. This will determine how much good time they will give you back at the Time Allowance Committee.

Do the best that you can to stay away from catching Tier III's because tier three's affect everything. Tier III's will stop your area preference transfer, which is simply a transfer to a hub of your choice closer to your family and the area you are from. Tier III's can ruin your Family Reunion Program visits, and for those who don't have a lot of time to do, tier three's will affect your participation in those programs that will assist you in getting out of the door a lot quicker, such as C.A.S.A.T., L.C.T.A., and Work Release. These and other programs will be discussed in another section of the book. This level of offense can be appealed to the Commissioner.

PROGRAMS

I n the earlier part of this book I explained to you about the programs that will be recommended to you through your counselor, established by Albany. These programs are recommended for you to take to assist you with your transition of getting in and out, for those of you that are not faced with a lot of time. For those of you that are faced with a lot of time, you will eventually take these recommended programs, but they will be given to you strategically throughout your period of incarceration. There are some programs that your counselor <u>will</u> <u>not</u> tell you about that will increase your chances of going home sooner and I will expound on those, but first I am going to bring your attention to the programs that were recommended to you by your counselor.

<u>RECOMMENDED PROGRAMS</u>

Upon arriving at your receiving facility/prison, the first thing you are going to go through is an orientation. Every orientation is ran differently for there is no set formula on how orientations are run in every prison/facility, but to give you a general idea as to what to expect at orientation it will mainly consist of you receiving an orientation handbook, of whatever prison/facility you are in, perhaps a rule book, and you will be informed of the types of programs that the prison/facility has to offer. You'll be able to figure out, to yourself of course, the type of program that you would possibly be interested in, and most definitely one that would more than likely teach you something. I highly recommend that if you have some time to do, to learn a trade/skill that you can take back to the street with you. Whatever it is that you choose it doesn't matter because there are some prisons/facilities that have a lot of programs to offer, just make sure you choose something that will place you in a decent marketable position upon your release because your main objective is to stay out there, and what better way to do so than by having a skill that is compatible with the current job market to assure you employment upon release. Your focus has to be on the things that will keep you out there free, employed and with your families/loved ones.

While you are going through this orientation stage, this will be marked down as a completion of one of the recommended programs that you will have to take. Let me rephrase that because you don't have to take any programs. You can refuse any program you wish to refuse, but keep in mind that when you refuse a program it will only hurt you in the long run. Some programs that you refuse, were you to choose to do so, will definitely be notated in your counselors folder as "Refusal of Program." This is only applicable for a recommended program, for a refusal of program can affect those of you that don't have a Conditional Release date (C.R.), or a better understanding of this is those of you that may have an indeterminate sentence. An example of an indeterminate sentence is a One to Three, Two to Four, Three to Life, Ten to Life, etc, etc,. Any sentence that has a number in the front (Minimum), and a number in the back (Maximum) is an indeterminate sentence. I am not one hundred percent sure if indeterminate sentences are still being given by the courts, because in 2005 the law was changed to where everyone is now being given determinate sentences (Flat bids). An example of a determinate sentence is a One and a half flat, Ten flat, Eighteen flat, etc, etc,. A determinate sentence is where you will have to do eighty five percent of your time and you will already have your date determined for you by Albany. On the contrary, with an indeterminate sentence you have to appear before the parole board four months prior to your minimum period is met (the number in the front), and on a determinate sentence your paper work goes before the parole board, not you physically. Having a determinate sentence you can still ruin your chances of early release by refusing programs, outrageous disciplinary records (i.e., constant fighting, assaults of staff or other prisoners, possession and usage of drugs, possession of weapons, etc.), just to name a few. Both indeterminate and determinate sentences carry some sort of supervision. With an indeterminate sentence you will have parole, and with a determinate sentence you will have post release supervision, where you will be supervised after release. Getting back to the programs.

PHASE ONE

After completion of Phase One which is your basic orientation/ introductory phase, and it consists of you being informed about the prison's/facility's administration, and the types of programs available in that prison/facility. Shortly thereafter, you will be called to see your counselor who will express to you that there are certain program needs that you must participate in either because of your criminal history, or your current conviction, or because of something that is mentioned by you in your pre sentence report (P.S.I.). Some of those programs that I am referring to are sex, drug and behavioral programs. I will elaborate on those programs that will be recommended to you that would be advisable to not refuse because a refusal can and will affect you being released. Phase One is a mandated two week paid program.

PHASE TWO

This is the core foundation phase, and it consists of a sequence of courses designed to provide prisoners with the skills necessary for living a productive and crime free life in society. Phase Two is mandated consisting of one paid module for the eight weeks.

PHASE THREE

This is the transitional phase that includes a total review of each persons progress during incarceration, and the development of a portfolio for each prisoner participant to take back to the community. Phase Three is a mandated six week program consisting of one paid module, and ninety contract hours for satisfying completion. This is the phase you go through once you have a release date and are heading out the door shortly thereafter.

ALCOHOL, SUBSTANCE ABUSE TREATMENT (A.S.A.T.)

Offered in mostly all prisons/facilities, and in all maximum security prisons you will be moved to a certain tier/gallery/company that is designated solely for those that are participating. In medium security facilities everyone that is programmed to A.S.A.T. will all be housed in the same housing unit. This program which is a therapeutic program, will be recommended to you by your counselor if you have a history of using drugs which might've been mentioned in your P.S.I. report or, you have a drug related crime or, during the course of your period of incarceration you have either been found guilty of a dirty urine and/or possession of drugs. Either way you will have to take this program if it is one of the recommended programs that Albany feels would suitably meet your needs of satisfactory program accomplishments to assist you with rehabilitation and getting out of prison. This program is a six month program that consists of mental exercises, experience sharing, group meetings/discussions, and is a structured environment that consists of a hierarchy that runs the housing area, as well as, the program along with the staff advisors who are not only civilians, but who are more than likely recovering addicts as well.

RESIDENCE SUBSTANCE ABUSE TREATMENT (R.S.A.T.)

The same as A.S.A.T., and is basically the same curriculum that outlines the "in house" concept of the familial structure of the A.S.A.T. program. There are some prisons/facilities that didn't require for you to be in the same housing unit or on the same gallery/tier/company to participate in the A.S.A.T. program. This revised edition removes that flaw so to speak, and everyone is placed in the same housing unit. Unlike the A.S.A.T. program that is only six months long, the R.S.A.T. program is eighteen months long.

AGGRESSION REPLACEMENT TRAINING (A.R.T.)

This is a program designed to assist us to be able to identify and control aggressive behaviors. The program is run by trained prisoner facilitators under the supervision of a facility staff coordinator. A.R.T. requires 100 hours (90 days) of participation, as well as, homework assignments designed to reinforce the newly thought techniques for controlling anger and aggression, and this program is offered to english and Spanish speaking prisoners.

CHEMICAL AND SUBSTANCE ABUSE TREATMENT (C.A.S.A.T.)

I placed this program with recommended programs because even though this may be a program that will not be a recommended program established by Albany, but this program can be mandated by the courts meaning that you will have to take it. This program is just a high intense version of A.S.A.T., but the difference is that in most cases once you've completed the therapeutic part of C.A.S.A.T. you will be entitled and approved to go to Work Release. However, as previously mentioned, if you were court mandated for C.A.S.A.T. and are approved for C.A.S.A.T., on a facility and then Albany level you will go to C.A.S.A.T., but you will not go to Work Release because yours was court mandated, and once you've completed the therapeutic part of the program you will be returned back to the facility that you came from. The good thing about it is that it would more than likely look good when you do appear before the parole board.

VOLUNTARY PROGRAMS

There are other programs that are of the voluntary nature, and are probably worth mentioning, but in my opinion are very valuable and at the same time don't count for anything. The voluntary programs you have are:

NARCOTICS ANONYMOUS (N.A.) English and Spanish
ALCOHOLICS ANONYMOUS (A.A.) English and Spanish

Why I personally feel that most do not count for anything is because it is your problem/addiction and you are supposed to do something to address your problem. Therefore, don't expect for the parole board or anyone else for that matter to view you more favorably in any aspect because you participated in voluntary programs that assisted you in addressing your problem/addiction. This is something <u>you</u> are supposed to do if you really want to help yourself, and then, if this is the case, it won't matter what any one says or thinks because at the end of the day, you participated because you wanted to help yourself.

<u>ALTERNATIVE TO VIOLENCE (A.V.P.)</u>

This program is sponsored by the Quakers, which is an outside organization, and this is a three day program (usually lasting an entire weekend), consisting of certain exercises, role playing, affirmation posters, light and livelys, etc., that are facilitated by outside facilitators and prisoners. At the end of this three day program you are given a certificate within a color scheme ranging from green, yellow, purple to gold, with gold making you eligible to become a facilitator.

<u>PRISONERS FOR AIDS COUNSELING AND EDUCATION (P.A.C.E.)</u>

This is a program where prisoners, staff and volunteers come together to cope with the HIV/AIDS epidemic through educational workshops and seminars. With the latest information/ statistics from the Center for Disease Control (C.D.C.), P.A.C.E. provides education of who HIV/AIDS is affecting, high risk areas, and the prevention of HIV/AIDS is affecting, high risk areas, and the prevention of HIV/AIDS. There is also very valuable information that you will be able to pass on and share with your families and loved ones to assist in educating them as well. This program lasts approximately four months consisting of different cycles, and at the completion of this program there is a certificate given as well. The ultimate goal of the staff facilitating this program is to encourage it's participants to become facilitators.

PROGRAMS THAT TEACH YOU SKILLS

In mostly all prisons/facilities you have programs that will give you the tools that you will need to place yourself in a decent marketable position upon returning back to society. Once you have acquired the skills needed that will increase your chances for employment, then you have not only taken advantage of the time that you had to do, but you took advantage of the programs that were available to you to assist you with survival once released.

As I said, most prisons offer these programs, and you'll find everything from General Business, Drafting, Carpentry, Plumbing, Electrician, Food Service, Barbering, Masonry, Radio and T.V. repair, Custodial Maintenance, Welding and Asbestos, the list goes on. There are some of these programs that teach you a skill that will qualify you for certification with the Department of Labor, but you'll have to check into which ones and how long you will have to participate in the program you choose to receive certification. You can find out by writing to the Department of Labor at:

N.Y.S. DEPT. OF LABOR
12 NYS CAMPUS
ALBANY, NEW YORK 12240

In every maximum security prison you have Corcraft industry, that allows you to be able to make some decent money as long as you are in the industry program. The industry programs are the highest paying jobs in every maximum security prison, and there aren't many medium security facilities that carry the industry program. There was Arthurkill with the Department of Motor Vehicle (D.M.V.) program that recently closed down, then you have Walkill with the Optical program, and Fishkill has an industry as well making beds. Off of the top of my head these are the only medium security facilities that I know of that offer the industry program.

The industry program allows you to make decent money because it is the most highest paying job in prison. For those of you with families/loved ones and especially children, being in the industry helps you to not only be able to stand on your own two feet as a man, but it takes the burden off of your families and loved ones. Most guys get into the industry and do the majority of their bid there while saving their money, and end up going home with a nice piece of change. Then you have some guys that help out their families by assisting with bills, paying for the trailer visits, etc., which is again, removing the burden off of your families/loved ones. Industry workers are paid on an incentive wage basis. Based on the pay scale where you are started off at the bottom and work your way up, but if say for instance your normal two week pay is twelve dollars and for that week the industry your in received a 100% bonus based on productivity output for that two week period, then for that two week period your pay would be double ($24.00). Which is pretty good because as you increase up the pay scale you make more and more. When I was in the tailor shop in Dannemora I would make $160 most month whenever we had the 100% bonus, which is excellent for being in a State prison where some guys are making six dollars every two weeks or twelve dollars a month. Check with your counselor when you get to wherever prison/facility you are in to see if they offer the Corcraft industry and how you can go about being assigned to the industry. If you have mandatory programs that you <u>must</u> take then you will not be allowed to participate in the industry program until those mandatory programs are completed. Again, check with your counselor.

For those of you that wish to further your education there are very few prisons/facilities that offer the college program. You have Sing Sing that offers the Master's Degree Program in

Theology, and you'll have to check with you counselor to find out what prisons/facilities offer college programs. If you are in a prison/facility that doesn't offer the college program, you will still be able to further your education, but it will have to be done independently. Whatever prison/facility you are in simply write to the Educational department and express your desire to continue your education, and he/she will inform you of your options, as well as, the cost of accomplishing such a goal. There are still a few maximum security prisons, as well as, medium security facility's that do offer college courses, but be sure to find out through your counselor what prisons/facilities offer further education, and how you can be able to participate.

PAROLE, AND OTHER FORMS OF RELEASE

The system as developed in 1977 was that the parole board would set a minimum sentence, and once that minimum sentence was set, the expectation in most instances was that the prisoner would be released on parole. Under then Governor Carey, the Division of Parole was separated from the Department of Correctional Services, and the only felonies that the parole board did not have the authority to set were A1 and A2 felonies.

However, in 1980 the responsibility for setting the minimum sentence was taken from the parole board and placed back within the sentencing courts, because on the legislature memorandum at the time was that there was absolutely nothing that the boards decision could possibly be based on that was not placed before the courts at sentencing.

The guidelines were then changed in 1985, where the focus consisted of only two factors, (The seriousness of the crime and Criminal history). Part of Section 259-i, the section governing periods of imprisonment, and 259-i(2)(c), the section governing discretionary parole release decisions, were the very factors that the legislature determined that the parole board should not be applying. As of this writing, these guidelines mentioned are still being applied today.

Under this scheme previously applicable, was that if a prisoner was appearing for the first time then there in effect was supposed to be a presumption of parole release. Release should be granted, unless one or more factors relating to institutional record and release plans were unsatisfactory. These guidelines used to permit a reasonable expectation of parole when a minimum sentence fixed in the courts with the guidelines has been served, provided the prisoner fulfills the requirements of the statute.

A parole board reliance on the severity of the offense to deny parole not only contravenes a discretionary scheme that is mandated by statute, but also constitutes an unauthorized re-sentencing of prisoners.

Recently there has been an amendment and improvement of the parole laws through a merger of the Department of Correctional Services and the Division of Parole, creating a new agency called Department of Corrections and Community Supervision. At the start of this merger was a repeal of Subdivision 1 of Section 259-i of the Executive Law, and secondly is the change of the Executive Law concerning factors that the parole board is now required to consider.

Under the new 2011-2012 amendment, a complete list of factors are now included in Section 259-i(2)(c), giving substance to the parole law. Most importantly is the inclusion of a focus of the parole board on the release plans of a prisoner, as well as, a risk-assessment that will now serve as a guide for the parole board that will more than likely have gone into effect within the month of January of 2012.

Section 259-i(c) now contemplates a different set of procedures that states that the parole board shall: "Establish written procedures for it's use in making parole decisions as required by law." This procedure shall incorporate risk and needs principles to measure the rehabilitation of those appearing before the parole board, and the likelihood of success of such people upon release. This was put in place to assist the members of the State Board of Parole in determining which prisoners may be released to parole supervision. This allows the parole board to be able to focus primarily on who the person is today, and whether or not that person can succeed in the community after release, as opposed to the previous guidelines that were based on who the person was many years ago when the crime was committed.

There are other forms of release as well, that apply to indeterminate and determinate sentences, and I will expound on those briefly.

The new Department of Corrections and Community Supervision has assumed responsibility for supervising prisoners after they are released from prison. All such forms of supervised release are now collectively referred to as "Community Supervision" within the relevant statutes, see: §1-a (amending New York Correction Law §2, to add a new subdivision 31: "Community Supervision" means the supervision of individuals "released into the community on temporary release, presumptive release, parole, conditional release, post-release supervision or medical parole"). There is one more form of release that is not mentioned here, and I will expound on this first.

LIMITED CREDIT TIME ALLOWANCE (L.C.T.A.)

There is not much relief for those of us with Life sentences for we are not eligible for Merit Time Allowance. We are not eligible for Presumptive Release consideration, and within the last ten years I haven't heard nor seen a person with life get Work Release/Furloughs. For those of you with life, there is the hope of L.C.T.A., which allows you to be paroled six months before your parole eligibility date, and I will explain to you how this works. Before continuing, know that L.C.T.A. is not just limited to lifers only, and can be applicable to anyone that meets the criteria, which is why I will explain it to you the first timer.

In order to qualify for L.C.T.A. consideration, there is a criteria that must be met based on your significant programmatic accomplishments. The next group of programs that I will mention, at least one of these must have been completed during your current term of incarceration in order to be reviewable. They are:

1). A minimum of two years of successful participation in college programming where the minimum standard should be six credit hours per semester, for a minimum total of 24 credits.

2). A Master's of Professional studies degree issued at Sing Sing, that calls for the successful completion of the New York Theological Seminary, Masters of Professional Studies program.

3). Attainment of a New York State Department of Labor Human Services Vocational Apprenticeship Certification.

4). Successful participation in the Puppies Behind Bars program consisting of a minimum of 16 months as a puppy handler or alternate puppy handler, and completed one or more of the following Penn Foster Certificates: Dog Obedience Trainer/Instructor, Pet Groomer, Veterinary Assistant.

5). A minimum of two years successful work as an Inmate Hospice Aide, after having completed the Hospice Aide Training program and served in the capacity of a Hospice Aide for two consecutive years.

6). A minimum of two years of successful participation as an Inmate Program Assistant (I.P.A.), at least one module a day in one of the following titles:

a). Academics Teacher's Aide
b). Vocational Teacher's Aide

c). Chaplain Aide
d). Program Aide II
e). Transitional Services Director
f). Case Work Supervisor
g). A.R.T./Transitional Services Facilitator
h). HIV/AIDS Peer Educator

The satisfaction of an L.C.T.A. program requirement requires two years of participation therefore, it is not possible for prisoners with less than two years in the departments custody to be granted an L.C.T.A. certificate. Once this two year requirement is satisfied your name will appear on a list held in the prison/facility law library. You can write to your counselor and inquire as well.

Along with the two year minimum in custody as a requirement to be screened, eligible A1 or persistent offender prisoners serving an indeterminate term with a life maximum and have previously appeared before the parole board, are considered reviewable when there is no recommended loss of good time either five years prior to the recent or future review date, rather than within the five years prior to their L.C.T.A. date.

A review by the facility L.C.T.A. Committee will be required, and prisoners with a maximum date of Life are reviewable upon completion of five years without receiving a recommended loss of good time.

A person is eligible for L.C.T.A. consideration if he/she is serving:

1). An indeterminate sentence for a non drug A1 felony such as Murder in the Second degree;
2). A determinate or indeterminate sentence for a violent felony offense as defined in Subdivision 1 of Penal Law section 70.02; or
3). A determinate or indeterminate sentence for an offense defined in Article 125 of the Penal Law.

A person is not eligible for L.C.T.A. consideration if:

1). You are serving a sentence for Murder in the First degree, or any Sex Offense defined in Article 130 of the Penal Law or an attempt or a conspiracy to commit such an offense;

2). You have ever filed a Civil action, proceeding or Claim against a State Agency, Officer or Employee that was found to be frivolous;

3). You are past your earliest Conditional Release date (if you are not serving an indeterminate sentence with a Life maximum term);

4). You are presently at DOCS pursuant to a Revocation of your Presumptive Release, Parole, Conditional Release or Post Release Supervision and have not been sentenced to an additional indeterminate or determinate term;

5). Any other offense for which a Merit Time Allowance is not available pursuant to Correction Law 803(1)(d).

To qualify for L.C.T.A. you must meet the following program and disciplinary criteria:

a). You must successfully be pursuing your Recommended EEP/Program Plan.

b). You must have completed a Significant Program Accomplishment as outlined in Section II (B) of the L.C.T.A. application.

c). You must not have been found guilty of any serious misbehavior during this current term of incarceration. Your overall disciplinary history will be subject to review to date, substance and number of incidents.

d). You must not have received any recommended loss of good time for the five year period before your L.C.T.A.

date. Recommended loss of good time before then will be subject to review by the facility L.C.T.A. Committee.

Again, as previously discussed you can find out more, and see if your eligible by asking your counselor or the prison/facility law library to find out if your name is on the list.

Recently the New York State Legislature enacted amendments to the Correction Law §803b, including additional program criteria that will qualify a prisoner for L.C.T.A. consideration. These recent amendments are effective immediately, in addition to the already established program criteria. Eligible inmates may be considered for L.C.T.A. consideration if they:

> Successfully worked in the Correctional Industries Optical Program for a minimum of two years and received a Certification as an Optician from the American Board of Opticianry.

> Received an Asbestos Handling Certificate from the Department of Labor upon successful completion of the training program and then worked in the Division of Correctional Industries Asbestos Abatement Program as a Hazardous Materials Removal Worker or Hazardous Materials Removal Group Leader for a minimum of eighteen months.

> Successfully completed the course curriculum and passed the minimum competency screening process performance examination for Sign Language Interpreter, and then worked as a Sign Language Interpreter for deaf inmates for a minimum period of one year.

Anyone who has met one or more of the above mentioned program requirements, and has previously submitted an L.C.T.A. application, and was denied based on L.C.T.A. program criteria not being satisfied, can request an L.C.T.A. application through their counselor and resubmit a new application. Further information regarding L.C.T.A. information can be found in your prison/facility's law library.

PRESUMPTIVE RELEASE

Under Title 7 of the New York Codes, Rules and Regulations, Chapter XXII, there is Presumptive Release, which also falls under Correction Law §806 and Department of Correctional Services Directive #4971, allows prisoners that are convicted of certain non-violent felonies to be released by the Commissioner of the Department of Correctional Services at their Merit time or parole eligibility dates without appearing before the parole board for release consideration. Note that the Department of Correctional Services makes the decisions about Presumptive Release and not the Board of Parole. If granted, Presumptive Release by the Department of Correctional Services you will only have to appear to sign the conditions of release. Prisoners are not eligible for presumptive release if they have committed felonies that are listed under Department of Correctional Services Directive #4791-§III B. Nor will a prisoner be eligible for presumptive release if he has been found guilty of a serious disciplinary infraction (Tier III), as provided under Directive #4971-§III C. You must successfully have participated in all assigned programs and have received an Earned Eligibility Certificate (EEP).

MERIT TIME ALLOWANCE

A person may actually be released prior to serving the minimum sentence if that person is incarcerated for a crime that qualifies for "Merit Time." Merit time is one sixth of the minimum sentence, so a person who is eligible for Merit Time appears before the parole board after having served five-sixths of his/her minimum sentence according to New York Correction Law §803.

Providing a prisoner who is incarcerated for certain non-violent crimes that fall under the guidelines specified in Corrections Law §803, 806 and the Department of Correctional Services Directive #4790, those prisoners are eligible for Merit Time release based on the above mentioned criteria. To become eligible for Merit Time there are certain crimes that you can not have been convicted of underlined in Directive #4790. §II A, and not found guilty of a serious disciplinary infraction as outlined under Directive #4790 §II B. You must have participated successfully in all recommended programs, and must accomplish at least one of the following:

i)   Get a G.E.D.
ii) Receive an Alcohol and Substance Abuse Treatment Certificate
iii) Receive a Vocational Trade Certificate following at least six months of programming; or
iv) Completed at least 400 hours of a Community Work Crew.

If you are eligible for Merit Time release, it will be determined by the Department of Correctional Services, and if so, you will appear before the parole board for Merit Time release prior to your regularly scheduled initial parole board appearance. Merit Time Allowance is applicable to both Indeterminate and Determinate sentences.

INDETERMINATE SENTENCES

The eligibility of Merit Time can reduce one's minimum sentence, who may have an indeterminate period of incarceration. If the Department of Correctional Services has determined that you qualify for Merit Time, you will be eligible for release based on this determination after serving only 5/6ths of your minimum sentence, according to New York Correction Law §803. If you are incarcerated for an Al non-violent felony for, as an example, Criminal Sale of a Controlled Substance with a maximum of Life, and are Merit Time eligible, you will be eligible for release after serving 2/3rds of your minimum sentence, for you are not eligible for Conditional release as someone sentenced to a Determinate sentence. If you have an Indeterminate sentence with a number on the back of your sentence other than Life and meet the criteria according to the Department of Correctional Services, you will be eligible for Merit Time release after serving 5/6ths of your minimum sentence and of a Conditional Release date of 2/3rds of your maximum expiration date.

DETERMINATE SENTENCES

If you have a Determinate sentence, and as I've previously explained to you that your Conditional release date is already determined for you, where you more than likely will not have to appear before the parole board, but your paperwork will after having served 6/7ths of your sentence. If the Department of Correctional Services determines that you are eligible for Merit Time release, it will be done after having served only 5/7ths of your sentence. For instance, if you have a fourteen year sentence for Criminal Sale of a Controlled Substance and are eligible for Merit Time release, you will be released after serving 5/7ths of fourteen years which is ten years, in comparison to the twelve years that you would have to serve for your Conditional release of 6/7ths of fourteen years.

SUPPLEMENTAL MERIT TIME

There has been additional Merit Time designed by Legislature for certain drug offenders called Supplemental Merit Time by the Department of Correctional Services, which is a part of the Drug Law Reform of 2004.

Supplemental Merit Time is only applicable to drug offenders with indeterminate sentences with the exception of Al drug offenders. Supplemental Merit Time can be found in §30 (1) of Chapter 738 of the Drug Laws of 2004, and can not be found in any statute. These laws state that:

> Every person convicted of a felony that is defined in Article 200 or 221 of the Penal Law, other than a Class Al felony offense defined in Article 220 of the Penal Law, which was committed prior to the effective date of this section and sentenced to an indeterminate term of imprisonment pursuant to provisions of the law prior to the effective date of this section and who meets the eligibility requirements of paragraph (d) of Subdivision 1 of §803 of the Correction Law as it exists on the effective date of this section, may

receive an additional Merit Time allowance not to exceed one-sixth of the minimum term or period imposed by the court provided the inmate has either (i) successfully participates or has participated in two or more of the four programs set forth in paragraph (d) of Subdivision 1 of §803 of the Correction Law; or (ii) successfully participates in one of the programs set forth in paragraph (d) of Subdivision 1 of §803 of the Correction Law, and successfully maintains employment while in a Work Release Program for a period of not less than three months. Pursuant to Correction Law §805 which gives description as mentioned above of what eligible inmates must do to earn Supplemental Merit Time, as well as, Directive 4790, Section III (A)(2), and Directive 4791, Section IV (B), give the requirements to meet the qualifications for eligibility of Supplemental Merit Time.

WORK RELEASE

Under Article 26 of the Correction Law that covers eleven sections from §851 to §861 gives you an in depth understanding of what Temporary release programs are about.

Included within this above mentioned section of Correction Law are the procedures Albany provides along with a section of case law that is applicable to this section.

Things have changed so much regarding Work release, that you very rarely see people getting it anymore, even though it still exists. You still have to meet the range of Temporary release point system, which if I'm not mistaken is still 32 points.

Once you have the necessary points that qualify you as being eligible for Work release consideration your name will appear on a list that is circulated to each prison/facility by Albany, and you are then placed on a call-out to be seen for an interview. You will receive a decision after your interview, and if the facility approves you then you have to wait for it to go to Albany who nine times out of ten will agree with the approval on the facility level and you will go to Work release. If the prison/facility does not approve you, you can appeal to Albany, who can either reverse the facility's denial and grant Work release for you or affirm the facility's denial.

SHOCK INCARCERATION

As outlined in Article 26A of the Correction Law and Chapter 9 of the New York Codes, Rules and Regulations §8010, covered by Chapter XI and following within three Sections from §865 to §867.

Shock Incarceration is an alternative to incarceration for a first timer that has been sentenced, and if eligible, can possibly end up in Shock Incarceration which is completed within six months of participation that is required in the program, who in turn can end up on the streets after the six month completion in the Shock program. Section 1800.2 explains the eligibility of those completing the program for parole release, and Section 1800.3 gives you the composition and function of the Shock Screening Committee.

Shock can be recommended by the sentencing judge, but just because it may have been recommended by the sentencing judge doesn't necessarily mean that it would be given to you once you've come upstate. Always remember that once you are a part of this controlled environment, if anything at all can go wrong, it will. Those of you that this applies to can further educate yourself by getting into the law library and/or have your lawyer stay on top of them from the outside which could possibly require some litigation from your attorney.

IMPORTANT ADDRESSES
AND INFORMATION

I've explained to you how important your family members are to you throughout doing your period of incarceration. As a prisoner (those of you that have to do time), there are no two ways about it, you <u>must</u> educate your families as to the harsh treatment, the verbal and physical abuse at the hands of the prison guards, etc. In order for your families and loved one's voices to be powerful, the power in their voices only comes from insight and education. Hence, you will find enclosed the addresses and phone numbers to nearly all of the agency(s) in Albany that will be able to assist you and your families by making things a little bit easier for you throughout your period of incarceration. Remember you are only as powerful as your voices on the outside, and your voices on the outside's power only comes from your teaching and educating them. Do not lose this information because one day you just may need them.

Attorney General of the State of New York
The Capitol
Albany, New York 12224-0341

Department of Correctional Services
State Office Building #2
State Office Campus
Albany, New York 12226

Office of the Inspector General
Executive Chamber
State Capitol
Albany, New York 12224

Governor's Office
Executive Chamber
State Capitol
Albany, New York 12224

Office of the Commissioner
Building 2, State Campus
Albany, New York 12226-2050

Director of Special Housing
Correctional Facilities Operations
Building 2, State Campus
Albany, New York 12226-2050

Director of Employee Investigation Unit
Building #2, State Campus
Albany, New York 12226-2050

Deputy Commissioner for Program Services
Building 2, State Campus
Albany, New York 12226-2050

Kemp "Zac" McCoy

Director of Ministerial and Family Services
Building 2, State Campus
Albany, New York 12226-2050

Deputy Commissioner and Chief Medical Officer
Building 2, State Campus
Albany, New York 12226-2050

EPILOGUE

A
s expressed in the introduction to this book, this book was not written to glorify life in prison, because there is nothing nice about prison life. This life can turn a man into a beast, due to the survival mechanism that is automatically activated within most of us in order to make it in prison. Don't get it twisted though, if you don't have at least a pinch of ruthfulness, callousness and larceny within you, then that automatic mechanism will never be activated for most of you, because it is not who you are. On the flip side of that coin, this life can also scare a person straight, to the point of a man/ woman never wanting to commit crime again depending on what prison you end up being sent to, especially if it's a prison like Attica. Believe it or not, Attica was the one prison that I was in that stirred within me the frame of mind that I no longer want the street life (i.e., fast money, cars and women), and the mentality that goes along with it. No, this book is the total opposite of any type of glorification. This book was written with the hopes of being able to smack you back into reality so that you'll be able to learn how to appreciate your family, loved ones, life and liberty.

If your already in then hopefully, your on your way to reaching the point of feeling out of place. Hopefully, being in prison has begun to leave a bad taste in your mouth, as it has finally done me. It should bother you that you can't get up and go where you want to go when you want to. It should bother you that you can only go shopping for the things that you may really need, every two weeks. It should bother you that you can take a dump only at the times that are allowed by the Department of Corrections. It should bother you that you can't be with your wife/girlfriend/boyfriend/husband, children, family, etc., on a daily basis. If it hasn't started to bother you yet, then either you don't have enough time in or time to do, and you are not in one of those prisons/facility's that has a constant high tension rate, with a lot of stabbings and cuttings going on. Only when you reach that point where this starts to leave a bad taste in your mouth then, and only then, will you be able to say to yourself that you will <u>never</u> put yourself, and your family and loved ones through this madness again, and really mean and live it. If you don't already know this, then allow me to be the first to tell you that this is not a game. There are people losing their life at the hands of other prisoners on a regular basis. There are people losing their life at the hands of correction officers on a regular basis, and what's crazy about this is that they are politically connected in these little towns, and are able to get away with it. To give you a glimpse of some of the things that really go on in prison, read my first book entitled, **"BEHIND THE WALL"** which is based on life in prison where each and every incident is an actual occurrence, but the names and places were changed so as to not place anyone in any harm.

If you've gained absolutely nothing from this book after having read it, I urge you to at least walk away with this one piece of advice. Value your life and freedom as long as you have it, because once you are trapped in this system and you become a number, your life and freedom as you know it, no longer belongs to you, and will never be the same.